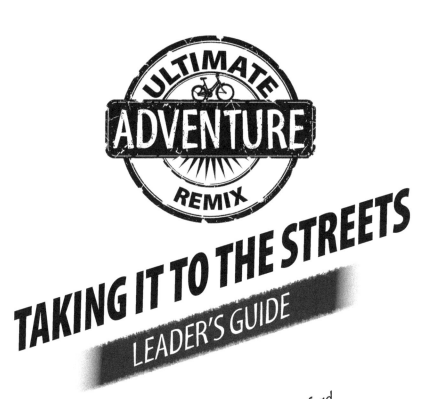

TAKING IT TO THE STREETS

LEADER'S GUIDE

by Andy Stephenson and Rick Winford

Warner Press

Anderson, Indiana

Coordinator of Publishing & Creative Services
Church of God Ministries, Inc.
PO Box 2420
Anderson, IN 46018-2420
800-848-2464
www.chog.org

To purchase additional copies of this book, to inquire about distribution, and for all other sales-related matters, please contact:

 Warner Press, Inc.
PO Box 2499
Anderson, IN 46018-2499
800-741-7721
www.warnerpress.org

Cover design by Morgan Clipner.
Text design by Mary J. Jaracz.
Edited by Kevin Stiffler and Stephen R. Lewis.

ISBN-13: 978-1-59317-535-1

Printed in the United States of America.

Contents

Welcome to

ULTIMATE ADVENTURE Remix

To say we are a little excited about this final level in Ultimate Adventure Remix would be a major understatement. We are pumped, ecstatic, jubilant, joyous—you get the drift. We are jumping up and down like we just won the lottery (no, we really don't play the lottery, but we would jump up and down if we won it!). This is where the rubber meets the road. We're excited because not only will your students be learning about God's mission for their lives, but they will be living it out.

This level is great for student leadership teams or college age students who really want to grow. The design is for students to not only talk about their life mission, but to experience it in an experiential way.

Taking It to the Streets alternates for twenty weeks between one week with a group session and student journal assignments and one week with a group project and self-directed student Bible study. You will help your students to immediately apply what they are learning by leading them on "Taking It to the Streets" group projects. Of all the levels in Ultimate Adventure Remix, this is the one that will require the most time, work, and maturity on your part and on the part of your students. For the final session, we suggest that you take your group on a biking trip. At the very least, have some fun together in celebration of what God is doing among you.

What you are about to experience will change your and your students' lives forever. We believe in what you're doing, and we believe in the generation of students you are discipling.

Committed to raising up an new generation of Christ-centered leaders,
Andy Stephenson and Rick Winford

Using
TAKING IT TO THE STREETS

Here are some suggestions to help you effectively promote, plan for, and teach *Taking It to the Streets:*

1   **Discuss your plans with your pastor.** Get him or her on board and praying for you.

2   **Review all twenty weeks of the Leader's Guide** (this book) before you begin. The more familiar you are with its contents, the less likely you will be to blow off course along the way.

3   **Recruit students for this series.** Do this several weeks in advance of the first session, with clear intent and with a sincere sense of excitement. If you just completed *Feeling the Wind* (Ultimate Adventure Remix 3), those students will be natural participants. If you are assembling a student leadership team for your youth group, this would also be a natural study for them to do. Be sure you communicate the date, time, and place that you will be meeting. Also suggest that students wear casual attire for the sessions.

4   **Carefully consider the size of your group.** Having more than twelve or so students may hamper openness and cultivation of the closeness that is more easily fostered in a smaller group.

5   **Be sure to order enough student journals** for each of your students to have a copy.

6   **Recruit at least one apprentice teacher**, perhaps more, to help throughout the series. If your students start reaching out to their peers and drawing in other teens as a result of this experience, you may need to expand the number of discipleship groups you

offer in the future. It will help to have leaders in training for this possibility. You can serve as a helpful model as your apprentices look ahead to the possibility of assuming primary responsibility for teaching at some point in the days ahead.

7 **Stress consistent attendance.** The sessions in this series are interrelated, and each builds on the previous one. This level of Ultimate Adventure Remix requires a higher level of commitment than the previous one. Students will need to complete assignments according to the following schedule:

Odd-numbered Weeks
- ⊘ Attendance at the group session
  A twenty- to thirty-minute devotional period five times a week
- ⊘ Completion of three "X-treme Challenges" from the student journal
- ⊘ Weekly memorization of a Bible verse

Even-numbered Weeks
- ⊘ Participation in the "Taking It to the Streets" group activity
- ⊘ Self-directed study of a large portion of a book of the Bible

8 **Pray for each student and his or her spiritual growth.** Don't forget this key element! If you flawlessly attend to all the other details and neglect this point, you will put all your time and energy into a journey that goes nowhere.

9 **Consider the length of individual sessions.** Each one is designed to last ninety minutes. You may need to make alterations to fit what works best for your group.

10 **Determine where you will meet for the group sessions.** You can opt to gather in someone's home, at the church, or wherever you find a place that is warm, welcoming, and inviting to teenagers.

11 **Prepare for the "Taking It to the Streets" group projects**
(even-numbered weeks) and the interactive activity in Session 20.
It would be ideal if you could take your students on a bike trip of
significant length, but you can also take them to one of the
following:

- ⊘ To an event that features biking or even motorcycle riding.
- ⊘ To a park, campground, a ropes course or someplace where
  you can enjoy outdoor activities.
- ⊘ To help clean up or fix up the home of a disadvantaged
  family or a section of your city or community.
- ⊘ To do yard work for someone who is homebound.
- ⊘ To assist at a local shelter or food bank.
- ⊘ To paint the home of an elderly congregation member.

Whatever activity you choose, try to plan something that
requires teamwork and cooperation. Even a pizza or pool party
could suffice if you are intentional about celebrating your
students' spiritual development and the ways in which their
shared life in Christ has been deepened by this series.

12 **As the leader, it is crucial that you thoroughly review the
material before each group session.** Use this book as a guide,
but express the thoughts and questions in your own words, in
ways that best suit your students.

PROSPECTIVE STUDENT LIST

Name:

Phone: E-mail:

....

Name:

Phone: E-mail:

....

Name:

Phone: E-mail:

....

Name:

Phone: E-mail:

....

Name:

Phone: E-mail:

....

Name:

Phone: E-mail:

....

Name:

Phone: E-mail:

....

Name:

Phone: E-mail:

....

Name:

Phone: E-mail:

....

Name:

Phone: E-mail:

....

Name:

Phone: E-mail:

....

Name:

Phone: E-mail:

....

Name:

Phone: E-mail:

....

Name:

Phone: E-mail:

....

Name:

Phone: E-mail:

....

Name:

Phone: E-mail:

....

Name:

Phone: E-mail:

....

WHAT IF?

What if you get to your group session and a student has not completed the individual "X-treme Challenges" or didn't show up for your last "Taking It to the Streets" group project? We strongly suggest that the issue be addressed in front of the whole group. If one student stayed up until midnight to stick with her commitment and another just blew it off, morale is quickly deflated by the team member who did not pull equal weight. Typically at this level you have student leaders who have invested in a high level of commitment. Let your students know that everyone needs to work together. It isn't fair to those who do the assignments not to give some extra project to someone who didn't fulfill the commitment. Here are some things you could possibly do in these situations:

- ✅ Assign some extra reading in a book you choose, twenty pages or so for each challenge not completed. Have the student write a short summary of what was read.

- ✅ Assign an extra project, maybe some work at the church or for someone in the church.

- ✅ Assign a video for the person to watch and write a short summary on.

- ✅ Give each student one or two "mercy passes" for the duration of the course. This would be a pass they could give to you if they didn't complete their assignment; there would be no extra assignments given to them. At those times you could tie in a comment about God's mercy to us. We suggest giving no more than two mercy passes to each student.

- ✅ Assign some extra scripture to memorize and quote in front of the class.

- ✅ Assign a book of the Bible to study and report on. (Make sure this is extra to the books and passages used for a student's personal Bible study on the even weeks.)

Be creative in how you deal with these situations, but do make sure you address them and be clear with your students that each member is expected to fulfill his or her commitments. You use your best judgment, yet our experience is if a person consistently doesn't fulfill their commitments, over time it brings the rest of the group down. You don't want to be the police and you don't want to be legalistic, yet at the same time if they were committed to play on a sports team they would be expected to commit to being at practices and games. Students are used to being asked to stick with commitment. At this level in the adventure, your students should be advancing in their spiritual maturity. Expect that from them. Because of the length of this course their will be some students who miss occasionally because of circumstances beyond their control. We suggest that you set a policy on how many absences they can have without consequences.

Understanding Your Life Mission: Family

OBJECTIVES

- To show the importance God places on the family.
- To help students understand how God wants them to interact with their families.
- To understand the mission God has for us in regard to our families.
- To pray for families.

Resources Needed

Bibles

Student journals, pens or pencils

Understanding Your Life Mission: Family

Warm Up

Welcome all participants to the opening session and give each one a student journal. Explain that *Taking It to the Streets* will require a high level of commitment and that for the duration of the series you expect them to do the following:

- ⊘ Block out five days on the odd-numbered weeks to spend twenty to thirty minutes studying God and his Word.
- ⊘ Spend time talking with God.
- ⊘ Work through the guided activities in their journals.
- ⊘ Memorize the memory verse on odd-numbered weeks.
- ⊘ Complete the three "X-treme Challenges" on odd-numbered weeks.
- ⊘ Participate in the "Taking It to the Streets" group projects on even-numbered weeks.
- ⊘ Study a large portion of a book of the Bible on even-numbered weeks, using the guide in the back of their journals.

Urge class members to seriously consider what they are about to promise to do. Review with them the "Introduction" section at the beginning of their journals. Ask those who are willing to commit to this study to complete the "My Commitment" covenant in their journals and turn it in to you. Those who are not ready to make such a commitment should be released after today's session with your blessing without being expected to attend future meetings.

Say, God will honor your commitment to grow closer to him by applying all he is teaching you.

Checking the Gear

Explain to students that during each of your future group sessions there will be a time when they will need to recite their memory verse; you will also be checking how they did with their journal assignments, including the five days of Bible study and the three "X-treme Challenges." You will also be checking that they did independent Bible study during the "group project" weeks (there is a guide in the back of their journals to assist them). For today's session, the Bible passages and questions are all included in Week 1 of their journals for their convenience.

Ask for volunteers to look up the following scriptures and read them to the class:

- ✅ Exodus 20:12
- ✅ Leviticus 19:3
- ✅ Ephesians 6:1–3

Invite students to summarize what these verses say. They all deal with proper and respectful treatment of our parents. Ask, *In light of what we just read, how do you treat your parents?* Invite students to respond.

Next, ask student to express their treatment of their parents on a scale of 1 to 10, with *10* indicating they are always trustworthy, respectful, honoring, and encouraging and *1* indicating that they never put these things into practice. Invite those who are willing to share what they put and why. If anyone answered lower than a *9*, what are some things they might do to improve how they treat their parents?

If time permits, you could also check out Proverbs 10:1; 15:20; and 23:22.

Starting the Course

Read together in Genesis 27:1–45 about two brothers who had some problems. Ask, *What happened between these two brothers?* Point out that Esau certainly had plenty of reasons to be upset with Jacob! Next, ask students to describe times when they were tricked or deceived by a brother or sister. Encourage them to also share some of the little everyday things their siblings do that get on their nerves. Now ask, *What are some things you do that get on their nerves?* If your students are honest, this is usually a two-way street.

Look up the following passages and discuss what God says there about relating to others:

- ✓ 1 John 2:9, 11
- ✓ 1 John 4:20
- ✓ 1 Timothy 5:1–2, 8
- ✓ Ephesians 4:29
- ✓ 1 Thessalonians 4:9

Point out that there are no conditions placed on this treatment. We don't act with love, respect, and patience when the other person has earned it or deserves it; we are to do it at all times.

Invite students to express their treatment of their brothers and sisters on a scale of 1 to 10, with *10* indicating they are always loving and encouraging and *1* indicating that they never put these things into practice. Those with multiple siblings can do multiple rankings; those without siblings can evaluate how they treat those closest to them other than their parents. Discuss responses. If anyone answered lower than a *9*, what are some things they might do to improve how they treat their brothers and sisters?

Running the Course

Say, *The Bible has a lot to say about families. In the Jewish custom the family tree was of incredible importance. Let's check it out.* Invite different students to look up Matthew 1:1–4, Exodus 6:14–15, Luke 3:23–26, and Numbers 1:5–9. This provides a small taste of the meticulous family lines recorded in the Bible. Explain that the Israelites were so concerned about carrying on the family name that if a man had a brother who was married and died without children, it was the living brother's responsibility to marry his sister-in-law and have a kid in his brother's name. If time permits, you can check this out in

Deuteronomy 25:5–6. Even today, God is still serious about our earthly families and how we interact with them.

Invite students to look up and read these verses:

- ⊘ Exodus 20:12
- ⊘ Ephesians 6:1–3
- ⊘ Leviticus 19:3
- ⊘ Proverbs 23:22

Ask, *What are these verses really saying?* We should show honor and respect to our parents. Encourage students to think of practical ways we can put these verses into practice.

Ask a volunteer to read Exodus 21:17. Say, *Aren't you glad this doesn't happen today? Half of us would be dead.*

Point out that proper treatment of our families also applies to our "extended" family—the family of God. Ask students to look up the following scriptures together. (You may want to look at them in unison and move from one to the next instead of assigning different students different ones):

- ⊘ Matthew 12:50
- ⊘ John 1:12
- ⊘ Romans 8:15
- ⊘ Ephesians 4:29
- ⊘ 1 Timothy 5:1–3
- ⊘ 1 John 3:1, 11, 14–15

Ask, *What are the main points of these scriptures?* We are children of God. When we accept Christ, we become brothers and sisters to all other Christians and should love each other. We should treat each other with respect and encourage each other. Explain that when we become Christians, we become part of an even bigger family, *the church.* (Your next group session will focus on this extended family.)

Say, *Let's wrap up this meeting by taking a deeper look at our immediate family.*

Finishing the Course

Invite students to look at "My Family in Week 1 of their journals and invite them to share their responses to the questions there. Encourage each student to share at least two or three times, and be sure to share your own personal thoughts:

- One of my favorite days spent with my family was...
- One of the funniest or fun experiences we had as a family was...
- One of the saddest times we had was...
- One of the things that I don't ever want to forget about my family is...
- One of the things I appreciate about my mom is...
- One of the things I appreciate about my dad is...
- One of the best things about my brothers and sisters is...
- In my family, I am truly thankful for...
- If there were one thing I could do to improve my relationship with my mom it would be...
- If there were one thing I could do to improve my relationship with my dad it would be...
- If there were one thing I could do to improve my relationship with my brothers and sisters it would be...

Explain that God has given us a specific mission for our families. We are to support and encourage each other. We need each other. To truly fulfill God's plan for us in our families, we should remember four things:

- Love—John 13:34, 1 Corinthians 13:4–5. Ask, *What does it really mean to show love? What are some ways we could put this into practice in our families?*
- Unselfishness—Philippians 2:3–5. Ask, *What does it really mean to be unselfish? What are some ways we could put this into practice in our families?*
- Respect—1 Peter 2:17. Ask, *What does it really mean to show respect? What are some ways we could put this into practice in our families?*

☑ Truthfulness—Colossians 3:9. Ask, *What does it really mean to be truthful? Is telling part of the truth, but not the whole truth, a form of lying?* Whether it's a big lie or a small lie, it is still a lie. To lead someone to believe something that is not entirely true is a form of lying.

Say, *Our mission is to exhibit all four of these in our families daily.*

Cooling Down

Take prayer requests for specific needs in your students' families. Maybe it is for one student to be more loving, for someone's parents to come to Christ, or for one of your students whose home life is not so good. Be sensitive to those whose families aren't healthy.

Give students the time, date, and details for next week's "Take It to the Streets" group project. Be sure to instruct them in the proper attire and to provide permission slips as necessary. You may want to make up a flyer they can take home that will provide the necessary information for them and their parents. Also be sure students know to be working on the Week 3 memory verse, five days of study, and three individual "X-treme Challenges," and the Week 2 individual Bible study over the next two weeks.

SESSION 2

"Taking It to the Streets" Family Project

Do something together as a group for someone's family. It may be a family in the church that needs some help, an elderly couple or widow, your pastor's family, or the family of one of the students in your group. Maybe a group member has a parent or grandparent with a long-term illness. Please remember that this is not a project to get one of your students out of his weekly lawn mowing job. The project could involve almost anything—cleaning out a garage, vacuuming the rugs, picking up leaves and limbs in the yard—whatever. Make sure that you set up the project in advance and that there is enough work to keep all your students busy for the designated time. Scheduling the work to be done on the same day and time as your group sessions may work best.

After your project is done, take your students to a quiet place and debrief the experience with them. Do this immediately afterwards instead of waiting until your next group session. Here are some questions you can use (feel free to add your own):

- What stood out to you as we worked together?
- What was really meaningful about this experience?
- How did you feel before we went?
- How did you feel after we finished?
- Did you really feel you were making a difference? If not, what could have been done differently?
- How do you think Jesus felt about our mission?

Before your students take off, remind them that you will be checking their Week 3 journal assignments (including the memory verse, the five days of study, and the three individual "X-treme Challenges") and checking in with their individual Bible study at your next group session.

Understanding Your Life Mission: Church

OBJECTIVES

- To understand God's view of the church.
- To understand how God wants us to be involved in our local church fellowship.
- To understand the importance of unity, passion, and service in the church.
- To pray for the local church body.

Resources Needed

Copies of church pictorial directory if you have one with pictures cut out; or scavenger hunt dealing with information about the church

Bibles

Student journals, pens or pencils

Session 3

Understanding Your Life Mission: Church

Warm Up

Option 1

Use one (or several) copies of a current church pictorial directory and cut out several pictures of singles, couples, or families that do not have any students in the youth ministry. Ask students to identify the pictures by name. You can do this as one group to see how many they can identify in five minutes or as teams pitted against each other. You can add extra challenge by using an older directory rather than a current one. (If you do not have a directory, or if your students already know everyone in the church, you may need to choose Option 2.)

Option 2

Before your session, prepare a list for a scavenger hunt using characteristics or information about the church building itself, such as the number of doors in the fellowship hall, the number of pews in the sanctuary, the brand of fire extinguisher in the hallway, and so forth. If your church meets in a school or other building, design some questions around that building or the neighborhood where you meet. You will also need to find the answers yourself before the session. Give each student the list and see who can get the most correct answers the fastest. Have them work individually or in pairs, depending on the size of your group. Give them a time limit of five to eight minutes.

After the activity, ask, *How well did you do? Better or worse than you thought you did?* Explain that this was a fun exercise to get focused on the church. Usually we think of the church as a building or a place we go, but it is really a group of people.

Checking the Gear

Have students recite the Week 3 memory verse (Ephesians 4:2–4) and make sure they completed the five days of study, the three individual "X-treme Challenges," and the individual Bible study. Spend some time getting specific feedback about the "X-treme Challenges." Were they difficult or uncomfortable to do? What feelings did they bring up? What was learned? Taking time to thoroughly process spiritual exercises and experiences will go a long way toward helping to bring about change and growth in the lives of your students.

Starting the Course

Say, *Our focus has turned to the early church—how it started, how the people dealt with each other, and how they turned one city completely upside down. As you studied in Acts, what were some of your reactions to what was going on?* Invite students to respond and to read or summarize their news stories from Day 1 and Day 2 in Week 3 of their journals. Ask,

What impressed you the most about these people? What event or occurrence was the most exciting to you? Invite students to respond.

Say, *Now let's discuss how we can influence our church to be more like the early church.*

Running the Course

Point out that there were three things that were very evident in the early church: *unity, passion,* and *service.* Ask students to give examples of each from their study of Acts. We suggest that you don't let them just recite the passage reference where they found the examples; ask

them to describe each example and why they included it in the list. Here are some possibilities:

- ✓ Unity—Acts 2:44, 2:46, 4:24, 4:32, 6:5
- ✓ Passion—Acts 2:43, 2:46, 3:1, 3:8, 4:31, 4:33, 5:41, 5:42
- ✓ Service—Acts 2:45, 3:6–8, 4:32, 4:34, 4:37, 5:15–16, 6:1

Finishing the Course

Say, *We've looked at how the early church stacked up when it came to unity, passion, and service. Let's discuss how we stack up.* For each of the following questions, try to develop actual discussion and conversation rather than just have a Q&A response. You don't need to have every student answer every question:

- 💬 First, let's discuss what we're doing right. What are the areas where you think our church is very unified?
- 💬 In what areas do you think we are very passionate about how we follow God?
- 💬 In what areas do you think we are doing a good job in serving others, both inside and outside the church?
- 💬 What are some areas where we are not very unified? or passionate? or service-oriented?

Be careful to prevent this from becoming a gripe-and-moan session about all the things that are wrong in your church. Steer students away from personal comments on individuals. Focus on the whole church and on issues, not people. (If necessary, point out that some people can still be passionate about worship even though they don't get into head-banging, drum-and-electric-guitar tunes.)

Invite students to share the ideas they have for helping to improve things in your church. Ask, *How can our group make this happen, or at least get it started?* Spend some time discussing and brainstorming how you can get this underway. Select one or two things and develop a schedule and a strategy to make it happen. Set a goal to see progress by the end of your study in *Taking it to the Streets*, and remember to pray about it a great deal.

Cooling Down

Spend most of your prayer time today praying for the issues in your local church, and how your group can be part of making progress.

Give students the time, date, and details for next week's "Take It to the Streets" group project. Be sure to instruct them in the proper attire and to provide permission slips as necessary. You may want to make up a flyer they can take home that will provide the necessary information for them and their parents. Also be sure students know to be working on the Week 5 memory verse, five days of study, and three individual "X-treme Challenges," and the Week 4 individual Bible study over the next two weeks.

SESSION 4

"Taking It to the Streets" Church Project

Talk to the church staff about something that needs to be done around the church. This should be a project appropriate for the skill level of your group and that can be started and finished at one time. Suggestions include:

- ⊘ Painting a Sunday school room
- ⊘ Cleaning out a storage building or closet
- ⊘ Cleaning, sorting, and fixing toys in the nursery

You might also check with the custodian and perform one of his or her weekly chores.

After your project is done, take your students to a quiet place and debrief the experience with them. Do this immediately afterwards instead of waiting until your next group session. Here are some questions use can use (feel free to add your own):

- 💬 What stood out to you as we worked together?
- 💬 What was really meaningful about this experience?
- 💬 How did you feel before we went?
- 💬 How did you feel after we finished?
- 💬 Did you really feel you were making a difference? If not, what could have been done differently?
- 💬 How do you think Jesus felt about our mission?

Before your students take off, remind them that you will be checking their Week 5 journal assignments (including the memory verse, the five days of study, and the three individual "X-treme Challenges") and their notes from their individual Bible study at your next group session.

Understanding Your Life Mission: School

OBJECTIVES

- To understand students' mission in their school environment.
- To understand God's emphasis on being witnesses for him in all parts of school.
- To pray for your students' schools.

Resources Needed

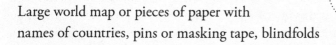

Large world map or pieces of paper with names of countries, pins or masking tape, blindfolds

Chalkboard or dry erase board

Bibles

Student journals, pens or pencils

Session 5

Understanding Your Life Mission: School

Warm Up

Before the session, post a large world map on one wall of your meeting room. (As an alternative, prepare twenty or so strips of paper with the name of a different country on each and post them on the wall in the general vicinity of where they would be on a world map.) Blindfold students one at a time. Spin them around several times and have them stick a pin or a piece of masking tape on the map (or assortment of countries). Once everyone has "selected" a place in the world, explain that they have been called by God to be missionaries to those countries. Encourage each student to creatively explain what kind of mission work he or she would want to do there, what kind of preparation it would take, and so forth. For example, Jason might "pick" Australia. Because he's a good basketball player, he decides he's going to start a Christian basketball camp program for inner-city kids. Encourage creativity and outside-the-box thinking.

Say, *A little creativity can go along way in sharing Christ with others.*

Checking the Gear

Have students recite the Week 5 memory verse (Romans 1:16) and make sure they completed the five days of study, the three individual "X-treme Challenges," and the individual Bible study. Spend some time eliciting specific feedback about the "X-treme Challenges." Were they difficult or uncomfortable to do? What feelings did they bring up? What was learned? Taking time to thoroughly process spiritual exercises and experiences will go a long way toward helping to bring about change and growth in the lives of your students.

Starting the Course

Remind students about Jesus' instructions to his disciples to be witnesses all over the world. He broke it down into four zones— Jerusalem, Judea, Samaria, and the ends of the earth. Even though you don't live in Jerusalem or Samaria, it's still possible to witness in the way Jesus intended. Ask, *What are the four "zones" where you can witness in your school?* To your closest friends (Jerusalem), to others who are like you (Judea), to the "tougher crowd" (Samaria), and to the adults who teach and administrate (ends of the earth).

Ask one or two students to read Peter's first sermon in Acts 2:14–41. Invite several students to share from their outlines of how they would explain the gospel (Day 1) and how their friends reacted to it (X-treme Challenge #1). Point out that when Peter shared with the people at Pentecost, he was taking to a large group of Jewish people who fully understood the terms and ideas he was using. However, often when Christians share the gospel they tend to use words and phrases that their audience *doesn't* understand. Ask, *What are some words and phrases we should avoid when talking to non-Christians about God?* Record students' responses on the board. Here are some suggestions to get them thinking in the right direction. These are not bad or wrong phrases in and of themselves, but sometimes the meanings are foreign to non-Christians:

- washed in the blood
- born again
- lamb of God
- eternal damnation
- lost in sin
- God incarnate

Now ask, *What are some words or ideas you could use to help non-Christian students better understand what you are saying about God?* Again, write students' responses on the board. Here are some possibilities:

- get to know God
- Jesus, God
- life totally messed up
- who became a man

Say, *Let's look at the people in our different "zones" more closely.*

Running the Course

Discuss the following questions, encouraging dialogue about each response:

- How many of your closest friends (your "Jerusalem zone") are Christians? How many are non-Christians?
- How often do you talk about God, religion, Christianity, or church with your closest friends?
- What group of people did you list as your "Judea zone," the people most like you?
- Do you think most people in that zone know that you are a Christian? Or would most of them be surprised to find that out?
- Who is in your "Samaria zone," the people you have a hard time loving? Why is it so hard for you?
- How much do you respect and appreciate the adults at school, in general?

Say, *Now that you are aware of these "zones" you can more effectively minister to the people who are in them.*

Finishing the Course

Direct students' attention to the Day 5 study of Week 5 of their journals. Point out again the fact that our witness to others consists of how we treat them and what it is we tell them about God. Ask for volunteers to share any experiences where they were mistreated by someone who claimed to be a Christian. Ask them how they reacted and how it made them feel. Say, *This just illustrates how important it is to treat people in a way that shows them we really care about them.* Now invite students to think about how well they are doing in this area. Are they improving, or do they still have a ways to go? Ask the group to relate any times where they have seen another member of the group doing something positive for people—in other words, doing the right thing.

Next, move to discussing how prepared students are to explain about their relationship with God. Ask, *How prepared do you feel to share Christ with others?* Depending on responses, you may want to spend time discussing what students need to improve their readiness. It might be more information, more confidence, more courage to start the conversation, or simply more practice in getting the right words down.

Say, *If you have thought about (and written out) the difference Christ has made in your life, you have already done a lot of preparing!*

Cooling Down

Ask the students to name all the Christian groups or clubs that are part of their school environment. This may include groups such as Fellowship of Christian Athletes, Campus Life, Young Life, First Priority, and so forth. Find out how many of your students participate in any of these. Ask, *Are these groups serious about Christianity on campus?* Most Christian groups on campus will be serious, particularly if they are part of a national structure or have an adult advisor. Encourage your students to check out these groups and to consider how participating in one could help students be stronger witnesses in their schools.

Take time to pray for any special needs in your group, and ask God to commission your students as witnesses in their schools.

Give students the time, date, and details for next week's "Take It to the Streets" group project. Be sure to instruct them in the proper attire and to provide permission slips as necessary. You may want to make up a flyer they can take home that will provide the necessary information for them and their parents. Also be sure students know to be working on the Week 7 memory verse, five days of study, and three individual "X-treme Challenges," and the Week 6 individual Bible study over the next two weeks.

SESSION 6

"Taking It to the Streets" School Project

Option 1

Meet with your students and help them create a plan to start a Bible study or Christian fellowship group at their school. Find out the appropriate administrators to ask. Plan a time and place to meet. (Will the group meet once a week before school? Every other week at lunch?) Decide on the purpose of the group. (Will the group focus on reaching out to students who don't know Christ? Will it focus on the strengthening and discipleship of those who already know Christ?) Have students work together to generate a list of names of other Christian students they can invite to help them start this group. The more student-led the group is, the better; do not feel that you need to be the driving force behind the regular meetings. Your primary role should be to find out what arrangements are necessary and help with them, and to lend support and guidance as needed. If you have group members in numerous different schools, this may be too large a project to tackle; you may wish to choose Option 2 instead.

Option 2

Make arrangements to travel to the schools represented in your group to pray for these schools and for the students who go there. If these campuses are open to letting you come on site, you might set up a meeting on a different day at lunchtime at each school. You could bring fast food to your students, if appropriate, but the main point is to gather with them and pray for their schools. Let the prayer time be led by your students. Be sure the prayers cover the different people and organizations within the schools. Include the principal and assistant principals, the counselors, the teachers, the athletic teams and the band and the debate team, the social clubs and the cheerleaders, and so forth. Ask God to bless them and for him to show you how to be an impact on each of the different people and groups you pray for. If you cannot go on campus at lunchtime, have your students meet you in the school parking lot after school or one evening.

Another idea is to ask the administration if you can do some type of service for them. Maybe wash lockers, clean windows, or do some other job that may need to be done but often doesn't get done regularly. Then after your service time, take time to pray for the school and those who attend. Be sure to make a flyer for your students letting them know when you will be where so they won't forget to meet you. If this works well, you may consider making it a regular part of your ministry.

After your project is done, take your students to a quiet place and debrief the experience with them. Do this immediately afterwards instead of waiting until your next group session. Here are some questions use can use (feel free to add your own):

- What stood out to you as we worked together?
- What was really meaningful about this experience?
- How did you feel before we went?
- How did you feel after we finished?
- Did you really feel you were making a difference? If not, what could have been done differently?
- How do you think Jesus felt about our mission?

Before your students take off, remind them that you will be checking their Week 7 journal assignments (including the memory verse, the five days of study, and the three individual "X-treme Challenges") and their notes from their individual Bible study at your next group session.

SESSION 7

Understanding Your Life Mission: Community

OBJECTIVES

- To understand God's view of our community.
- To understand how God wants us to live a lifestyle of servanthood.
- To help students understand how God wants them to interact with their community.
- To understand the mission God has for us in regard to our community.
- To pray for the community.

Resources Needed

Index cards (for Warm Up, Option 2)

Chalkboard or dry erase board

Bibles

Student journals, pens or pencils

Session 7

Understanding Your Life Mission: Community

Warm Up

Option 1

The object of this game is to say to the person next to you, "Who's your neighbor? Is Mrs. Mumble your neighbor?" without showing your teeth (it would be similar to having false teeth and having them out). The lips are pulled in over the teeth. The next person has to say "I don't know, you will have to ask my neighbor." The same guidelines apply, with no one showing teeth. If they both make it without showing their teeth, the process continues, with the previous person asked now asking the person next to him or her. This continues with persons sitting next to each other asking the question until someone shows his or her teeth by smiling or laughing; that person is then out. Stop when you feel the game has run its course.

Option 2

Have students write down on an index card the craziest thing they have ever had a neighbor do. (For example, I once saw my neighbor washing his car dressed in a ballet outfit.) Students should not sign the cards. Collect the cards and read them one at a time; students should try to guess whose neighbor you are referring to (three guesses max and then have them identify themselves). After you have matched the card with the person, let that person tell his or her story without mentioning names.

Say, *Today we will find out God's mission for us in our community, and who is really our neighbor.*

Checking the Gear

Have students recite the Week 7 memory verse (Matthew 22:37–40) and make sure they completed the five days of study, the three individual "X-treme Challenges," and the individual Bible study. Spend some time getting specific feedback about the "X-treme Challenges." Were they difficult or uncomfortable to do? What feelings did they bring up? What was learned? Taking time to thoroughly process spiritual exercises and experiences will go a long way toward helping to bring about change and growth in the lives of your students.

Starting the Course

Dig deeper with students about their experience ministering in their neighborhoods by discussing the following questions:

- What did you do?
- What were the reactions or results?
- How did it make you feel?

Some of your students may have encountered neighbors who were indifferent or even resistant to being ministered to. Ask, *Why would anyone not want someone else to help out in their time of need?* For some people, receiving assistance makes them feel embarrassed or guilty. For others, it's a matter of pride. And some people don't want things to "get better" because of the attention or ongoing assistance they get from their plight.

Say, *We don't have to go far to share the love of God; there are needs right outside our own door.*

Running the Course

Review with your students the story of the good Samaritan as found in Luke 10:25–37 and discuss the following questions:

🗨 *Why was it significant that the priest and Levite didn't do anything for the man who was hurting?* They were what we would call "church people." The priests were, and the Levites were assistants and helpers to the priests in the work of the temple.

🗨 *Why do you think Jesus used "church people" as examples of not helping?* If anyone should have been sensitive to this man's need and open to helping him, it was these two guys. Sometimes people just go through the outer motions of going to church or serving God, but inwardly their hearts are not changed.

🗨 *What was significant about a Samaritan helping a Jew?* The Jews disliked the Samaritans and were very prejudiced against them. They considered them to be half-breeds because they had intermixed with other races and were not fully Jewish.

🗨 *Why do you think Jesus used a "hated Samaritan" instead of a Jew to help?* Maybe he was trying to teach us a lesson about love and that we should treat all people the same.

🗨 *What major lessons do you think Jesus was trying to teach through this story?* God wants us to live out our faith and not just put on a show. God doesn't want us to be prejudiced but to love all people the same.

🗨 *According to Jesus, who is our neighbor?* Everyone with whom we come into contact.

Say, *The Bible talks a lot about helping others and taking the role of a servant.* Ask a volunteer to read Philippians 2:3–11. Discuss the following questions:

🗨 *What kind of attitude did Christ take?* Despite being God and ruler over all, he took the attitude of a servant and made himself nothing.

🗨 *What should we do in response?* We should have the same attitude that Christ Jesus had.

🗨 *What does this really mean for us today?* We should be willing to put others' needs before our own needs.

🗨 *Do you think most people live that way today? Why or why not?*

Now read together John 13:1–17. Ask, *Why do you think Jesus lowered himself to wash someone's smelly feet?* By doing this he showed us that *we* must be willing to humble ourselves to be used of God. Invite students to share about people they know personally who serve others with extreme humility and Christlike love.

Say, *Becoming like Christ involves more than just going to church and going through the motions. It means living like Christ by putting others' needs before our own.*

Finishing the Course

Ask, *What would it be like if Christians today had the same attitude as Christ in regard to their communities?* Neighbors would help each other out, prejudice would decline, and people would want to know more about Christ because they could see a difference in us. One of your students' "X-treme Challenges" for the week was to think of some needs of the people in the community and then think of some creative ways you and your group could show love to those people by helping to meet these needs. Ask, **What are some of the ideas on your list?** Write these ideas on the board, and discuss as a group how those ideas could be put into practice.

Now ask, *Have you ever been in a situation where you felt that really demonstrated the love of Christ to someone else?* Invite students to share about these times and the effect their actions had on others.

Cooling Down

Take prayer requests for specific needs in your local community. This might include praying for the next-door neighbors of one of your students who is sick or needs Christ or for protection for those in your town from crime and violence. You could even pray for those in the local community around your church building.

Give students the time, date, and details for next week's "Take It to the Streets" group project. Be sure to instruct them in the proper attire and to provide permission slips as necessary. You may want to make up a flyer they can take home that will provide the necessary information for them and their parents. Also be sure students know to be working on the Week 9 memory verse, five days of study, and three individual "X-treme Challenges," and the Week 8 individual Bible study over the next two weeks.

SESSION 8

"Taking It to the Streets" Community Project

Do something together as a group for the community. Here are some suggestions:

- Do a project for a neighbor of one of your students or maybe a neighbor who lives close to the church.
- Do something practical for the city or town you live in. Pick up trash in a park or wash car windows in a shopping center parking lot.
- Call the city manager or mayor's office and ask if there is anything your group can volunteer to do to help the community. Maybe you can help remove/paint over graffiti or sort books at the library.
- Do a prayer walk around the community near your church and pray for the houses in the neighborhood. Divide your group into pairs and give each a particular area to cover in prayer. As they walk, they can pray for the houses they are walking by and for those in them. As they walk, teams can pray out loud with their eyes open, in conversation with God and one another, taking turns praying for the houses they pass. The BLESS acronym can provide guidance:

  B—Pray for God's blessings for their bodies (health).
  L—Pray for their job (labor), for favor with their employers and so forth.
  E—Pray for their emotional needs, both individual and family.
  S—Pray for their social lives, that God would send strong Christians into their paths.
  S—Pray for their spiritual condition.

After your project is done, take your students to a quiet place and debrief the experience with them. Do this immediately afterwards instead of waiting until your next group session. Here are some questions you can use (feel free to add your own):

- What stood out to you as we worked together?
- What was really meaningful about this experience?
- How did you feel before we went?
- How did you feel after we finished?
- Did you really feel you were making a difference? If not, what could have been done differently?
- How do you think Jesus felt about our mission?

Before your students take off, remind them that you will be checking their Week 9 journal assignments (including the memory verse, the five days of study, and the three individual "X-treme Challenges") and their notes from their individual Bible study at your next group session.

Understanding Your Life Mission: Witnessing

OBJECTIVES

- To understand the why, when, and how of sharing Jesus with others.
- To help students understand how God wants them to interact with others.
- To understand the mission God has for us in regards to sharing the good news.
- To pray for individuals who don't have a personal relationship with Christ.

Resources Needed

Index card, small prize

Chalkboard or dry erase board

Bibles

Student journals, pens or pencils

Understanding Your Life Mission: Witnessing

Warm Up

Before the session, take an index card; write the words *Good News!* on one side and a message on the other. The message could be, *This card entitles your team to free soft drinks (or candy bars or whatever) after our meeting.* Divide your class into two teams (if you have three students or less, let them be their own team). Give instructions to find the "good news card" and bring it back for a reward. You can coach teams ("You're getting warmer! Or "You're really cold!") if they are having trouble finding the card. After the card is found, fulfill the reward if it is immediate (or give specifics of how it will be fulfilled later) and say, *Many people are looking for good news. Today we'll learn how we can help them find it.*

Checking the Gear

Have students recite the Week 9 memory verses ("The Romans Road"—Romans 3:23, Romans 6:23, Romans 5:8, and Romans 10:9) and make sure they completed the five days of study, the three individual "X-treme Challenges," and the individual Bible study. Spend some time eliciting specific feedback about the "X-treme Challenges." Were they difficult or uncomfortable to do? What feelings did they bring up? What was learned? Taking time to thoroughly process spiritual exercises and experiences will go a long way toward helping to bring about change and growth in the lives of your students.

Starting the Course

One of the Week 9 "X-treme Challenges" was for students to list three they know and have contact with who do not have a personal relationship with Jesus. They were supposed to pray for these people everyday day. Ask, *Did anyone find creative ways to remember to pray for the people on your list? Share with us some ideas?* Invite students to respond. Next, review with students Acts 16:22–34 and Acts 26. Point out that anywhere and anytime are right for sharing the good news of Christ.

Say, *Sharing Christ may not always mean making a speech and asking someone to pray with you, but you can always show kindness and pray for others.*

Running the Course

Say, *We've been using the term good news a lot. Just what is the good news?* The good news is that Jesus paid our penalty for sin by dying in our place. He wants a personal relationship with us, so we can be free from sin and have eternal life with him and live life on earth to the fullest.

Invite a student to read Luke 15:3–10. Discuss the following questions:

- *What do you think Jesus was trying to get across in these two stories—and how does it apply to us?* Jesus is very concerned about those who don't know him. Today he is much more concerned about us reaching the lost than he is with us being in a "holy huddle." We should be more focused on others than on ourselves.
- *If God is so concerned about those without Christ, what should be the church's main focus?* To reach the unsaved—and to help those who are saved grow so they can reach the unsaved.
- *Do you think most churches have this focus? Why or why not? What about our church?* It can be easy for churches to get comfortable and self-absorbed, losing their edge and their

passion to reach out for Christ. Ask your students to brainstorm with you about ways to help your church become more focused on those who don't know Christ.

Have the group look up and read Matthew 28:19–20 and Mark 16:15. Ask, *What should be our primary mission here on earth?* We are created to worship God and to share him with those who are lost. Once we get to heaven there will be plenty of time to worship God—but none left to share him with others! This fact should help the church set its priorities and focus.

Finishing the Course

Ask, *What would happen if all Christians shared a verbal witness? Would there be a difference in our world?* One of this week's "X-treme Challenges" had students write out their testimonies. Invite class members to share these stories with the rest of the group. As the leader, you may want to "break the ice" by sharing your testimony first. Praise your students for their efforts in focusing on their testimonies and writing them down—something that many Christians have never done!

Cooling Down

As a group pray, for the lost in your community. You may also want to pray for some of the names on the lists your students made. Pray that God would give each of you the courage and the chance to share with others.

Give students the time, date, and details for next week's "Take It to the Streets" group project. Be sure to instruct them in the proper attire and to provide permission slips as necessary. You may want to make up a flyer they can take home that will provide the necessary information for them and their parents. Also be sure students know to be working on the Week 11 memory verse, five days of study, and three individual "X-treme Challenges," and the Week 10 individual Bible study over the next two weeks.

SESSION 10

"Taking It to the Streets" Witnessing Project

Do something together as a group to share the good news with others in your community. Here are some suggestions:

- ⊘ Go to a busy street corner and hand out tracts about God's good news.
- ⊘ Get copies of the *Jesus* film and hand them out in a neighborhood. (Check out www.jesusfilm.org. You can get this movie for less than $10 a copy; there is also a version developed especially for children. You can even watch the video free on the website.)
- ⊘ If you prayer-walked the community a few weeks ago, go back and knock on the doors; tell the residents you are praying for them and ask if they have any specific needs you could pray about.
- ⊘ Go to a shelter or group home and have your students share their testimonies. (Be sure to make your intentions clear to the directors of these places first; many such organizations that are faith-based will gladly welcome you to do this.)
- ⊘ Have some of the students share their testimony at an event or activity.
- ⊘ Come up with another way to share Jesus.

After your project is done, take your students to a quiet place and debrief the experience with them. Do this immediately afterwards instead of waiting until your next group session. Here are some questions use can use (feel free to add your own):

- 🗨 What stood out to you as we worked together?
- 🗨 What was really meaningful about this experience?
- 🗨 How did you feel before we went?
- 🗨 How did you feel after we finished?

- Did you really feel you were making a difference? If not, what could have been done differently?
- How do you think Jesus felt about our mission?

Before your students take off, remind them that you will be checking their Week 11 journal assignments (including the memory verse, the five days of study, and the three individual "X-treme Challenges") and their notes from their individual Bible study at your next group session.

SESSION 11

Understanding Your Life Mission: Lifestyle

OBJECTIVES

- To understand how important our lifestyle is to our witness.
- To help students consider whether they have given God all areas of their lives.
- To challenge students to live a "no doubt" lifestyle.
- To pray for strength to live a lifestyle like Christ.

Resources Needed

Index cards, pens or pencils

Bibles

Paper

Student journals

Understanding Your Life Mission: Lifestyle

Warm Up

Write the names of at least five popular or well-known persons, one each on a different index card. These could include sports stars, movie stars, cartoon characters, politicians, or maybe your pastor. If you have a large group, ask if some students want to volunteer to do some acting. If you have a small group, let each student be a part of the acting. Give the first volunteer one of the index cards; this person then has thirty seconds to act out the person on the card as the audience guesses who is being portrayed. Time how long it takes the audience to figure it out. The actor who has his or her character guessed in the shortest amount of time is the winner. Let each person with an index card take a turn acting.

Point out that many people live life as actors or impersonators—trying to look like someone or something they are not. This is even true of some people who say they are Christians but live a lifestyle that doesn't match up with their words.

Say, *Today we will look at what it really means to walk the talk.*

Checking the Gear

Have students recite the Week 11 memory verse (Romans 12:1–2) and make sure they completed the five days of study, the three individual "X-treme Challenges," and the individual Bible study. Spend some time eliciting specific feedback about the "X-treme Challenges." Were they difficult or uncomfortable to do? What feelings did they bring up?

What was learned? Taking time to thoroughly process spiritual exercises and experiences will go a long way toward helping to bring about change and growth in the lives of your students.

Starting the Course

Your students "X-treme Challenges" this week all focused on self-analysis: considering whether God has full control of all areas of their lives, thinking specifically about whether the things they do glorify God, and asking someone they respect and trust to speak honestly about the integrity and consistency of the way your students live. Ask, *What did you discover about yourself? Whom did you speak to? What changes did you make?* Be honest about your own self-analysis. The goal is not for students to compare themselves with others, but to seek God's help in changing their lifestyles to clearly reflect his presence and activity.

Say, *A person's lifestyle will always speak much more loudly—and clearly—than his or her words.*

Running the Course

Read together Romans 12:1–2 and discuss the following questions:

- *What do you think it means when it says we are to be "living sacrifices"?* Our very lives should be lived in service to God. In the Old Testament, animals that were sacrificed ended up on the altar and were eventually killed. It is in some ways it may seem like a harsh concept, but we are to die to ourselves and be alive to letting God lead us.
- *Do you know people who say one thing and do another? How much respect did you have for them?*
- *What would you say to someone who said, "Christians are just a bunch of hypocrites"?* Christians are still human. People will fail you, but God never will. There are people in all kinds of professions who are fakes. That usually doesn't keep us from going to the doctor or from getting on an airplane, just because there are some cases where there are negative stories about doctors or pilots.

Read together Romans 12:2. Ask, *What does it mean to be transformed?* This means to become something else, totally different than before. Encourage students to share examples of people who have been transformed for the good, whose attitudes and actions have done a complete about-face.

Now invite someone to read aloud John 14:21. Say, *The best way to show that God has transformed our lives is by obeying his commands.*

Finishing the Course

Ask, *What would happen if all Christians really lived a lifestyle like Christ? Would there be a difference in our world?* Invite students to look up John 13:34–35 and 1 Corinthians 13. Ask, *What is the main theme of these two passages?* Love. When love is evident in the way we live, others will know that we belong to Christ. Showing love is more important than other good or even "churchy" things we could do.

During their Day 5 study, students were asked to think of specific ways to let the light of Christ shine through them at home, at church, at work, and "on the field" (everywhere). Invite those who are willing to describe the attitudes and actions that could make such a "shining light" possible.

Cooling Down

As a group pray that God would give all of you a love like Jesus' love for others. Pray that you will have the strength to live the kind of lifestyle that people will see Christ through.

Give students the time, date, and details for next week's "Take It to the Streets" group project. Be sure to instruct them in the proper attire and to provide permission slips as necessary. You may want to make up a flyer they can take home that will provide the necessary information for them and their parents. Also be sure students know to be working on the Week 13 memory verse, five days of study, and three individual "X-treme Challenges," and the Week 11 individual Bible study over the next two weeks.

"Taking It to the Streets" Lifestyle Project

Do something together as a group that will enable your students to share the good news with their lifestyle. Here are some suggestions:

- ☑ Call another church (even one in a different denomination) and volunteer your time as a group. A simple manual labor project could be effectively completed by your students. You might look in particular for a church that is small in number and does not have the manpower to do all that needs to be done around the facility. (Your pastor may be able to suggest a good place to call. Be sure that your offer does not come across as condescending but affirms your partnership with the receiving church in proclaiming the love of God.)

- ☑ If you really want to get radical and show Christ's love, call someone from a Hindu or Buddhist temple or a Jewish synagogue and volunteer the group for some manual labor. (Realize this is not an endorsement of any of these religions. Let your students know that. This is an attempt to show that Christ loves all people, even those of other religions. This effort of sacrificial love may be a seed that later opens dialogue or draws someone to Christ.) If you do this project, you may want to make sure you do some study about the particular region in comparison to Christianity so you can process it with your students.

- ☑ Do something for a neighbor around the church. Maybe there is someone who needs some help or a neighbor who gives the church problems by complaining frequently—do something for this person. Your pastor can help identify any likely candidates. Be sure you call and clear it with the neighbor first before starting the work.

- ☑ This idea is sneaky, but powerful. Take your group to the mall or someplace they can hang out for a couple of hours. When you get there, allow them some "free time." Arrange for one of your friends (unknown to your students) to have a "needy" moment in front of your students (e.g., car won't start, needs to make a phone call, trips and falls down). See how your students respond—does their lifestyle live up to their confession of faith? Afterwards, introduce your friend and explain to students what was going on.

After your project is done, take your students to a quiet place and debrief the experience with them. Do this immediately afterwards instead of waiting until your next group session. Here are some questions use can use (feel free to add your own):

- What stood out to you as we worked together?
- What was really meaningful about this experience?
- How did you feel before we went?
- How did you feel after we finished?
- Did you really feel you were making a difference? If not, what could have been done differently?
- How do you think Jesus felt about our mission?

Before your students take off, remind them that you will be checking their Week 13 journal assignments (including the memory verse, the five days of study, and the three individual "X-treme Challenges") and their notes from their individual Bible study at your next group session.

SESSION 13

Understanding Your Life Mission: Compassion

OBJECTIVES

- To understand how important compassion is to our witness.
- To challenge students to focus on what is on the inside rather than the outside.
- To pray to see people as Jesus sees them.

Resources Needed

Various supplies for Warm Up option

Bibles

Chalkboard or dry erase board

Paper, pens or pencils

Student journals

Understanding Your Life Mission: Compassion

Warm Up

Option 1

Prior to class take a candy bar, carefully open it at the seam, and remove the contents; in its place put a small wood block or other object the same size of the candy. Carefully reseal the wrapper. Also take a five-dollar bill and seal it in plastic. Place the bill inside a jar of dark-colored baby food, making sure that the bill cannot be seen from the outside. Put the lid back on the jar. Select a volunteer and tell this person that you have two gifts but you are only going to give out the one that he or she chooses. Show the candy bar and the baby food and let your volunteer choose (without touching the gifts). When the volunteer (hopefully!) chooses the candy bar, let him or her open it up. After the groans and moans of having a wood block instead of candy, reveal what was in the baby food jar. If the volunteer picks the baby food jar, don't panic; just jokingly say that your example has been destroyed, and threaten to spoon-feed the baby food to the volunteer.

Option 2

Before class take a small box, place a five-dollar bill in it, and wrap it like a present. Wrap it carelessly with the tape hanging off, the paper uneven, the ribbon off-center, and so forth—maybe even put some food stains on it. Also get some nasty (and fairly heavy) garbage and seal it tightly in a large plastic bag. Take a large box and wrap the bag of garbage beautifully and perfectly inside of it. Select a volunteer and tell this person that you have two gifts but you are only going to give out the one that he or she chooses. Show the small gift and the large gift; let your volunteer hold them and choose one. When the volunteer (hopefully!) chooses the larger gift, let him or her open it up. After the groans and moans of receiving a bag of garbage, reveal what was in the smaller gift. If the volunteer picks the smaller gift, don't panic; just jokingly say that your example has been destroyed and offer the garbage to the volunteer.

Say, *We can't always judge something by looking on the outside—including people. Today we'll explore some of the choices Jesus made when dealing with people.*

Checking the Gear

Have students recite the Week 13 memory verse (Colossians 3:12) and make sure they completed the five days of study, the three individual "X-treme Challenges," and the individual Bible study. Spend some time eliciting specific feedback about the "X-treme Challenges." Were they difficult or uncomfortable to do? What feelings did they bring up? What was learned? Taking time to thoroughly process spiritual exercises and experiences will go a long way toward helping to bring about change and growth in the lives of your students.

Starting the Course

One of the "X-treme Challenges" students were to complete was to focus for a whole day on being driven by love. In another Challenge they were to go out of their way to physically show love to someone they would usually not want to touch. Ask, *How did it go? Whom did you interact with? How did people react? How did you feel? Was it difficult or easy to live this way?* Encourage students to look at their journals and to report on what they experienced.

Say, *The things you did may have felt somewhat manual or forced, but Christ can change our hearts so that we sincerely desire to do these things.*

Running the Course

Ask students to pair up and give them the assignment to dig through the Gospels (first four books of the New Testament) and find instances of how Jesus dealt with people for who they were on the inside rather than the outside. Ask the pairs to write down the references and the summaries of what they find.

After 10–15 minutes, have students come back and report on what they found. Say, *Jesus defined compassion by what he said and did—he saw people for who they were on the inside and he loved them as is.*

Finishing the Course

Ask, *Why do you think Jesus was so concerned about the inside and so unconcerned about the outside?* He knew the inside is what will last, the real "us"; the outside (our physical bodies) will eventually die.

Invite someone to read Matthew 12:33–36. Ask, *What was Jesus trying to communicate in these verses?* What is on the inside will come out eventually; we can't hide it forever! Now invite someone to read Proverbs 4:23, 21:3, and 26:23. Ask, *What do these verses have to say to us?* What is on the inside is more important than what is on the outside.

As a group, brainstorm a list of things that people use to make judgments about others in our society (what they wear, how much they make, and so forth). Write students' responses on the board. Next, come up with things *Jesus* sees as important when looking at a person (attitude, love or lack of love for others, and so forth) and write these suggestions in a new list on the board. (Don't let anyone just say "The heart" without delving into what that means.) After you have your lists, discuss the following questions:

> *How many of you have a hard time looking at people for what is on the inside rather than the outside?* If we are honest this would probably be all of us.

🗨 *What are some ways we can do better at looking at others through Jesus' eyes?* Students might hold each other accountable each week, try to get to know someone before making a judgment, avoid stereotyping others, and so forth.

🗨 *What would happen if all Christians really saw people for who they were on the inside rather than the outside? What would happen if that were true of our youth group?* Invite students to respond.

Say, *When we look at others, our eyes should focus where the eyes of Christ focus: on the heart.*

Cooling Down

Ask each student to offer individual prayers to God that he would help them see people as Jesus does, for who they are on the inside rather than the outside. Close the prayer time by commissioning your students to be agents of compassion in their world this week.

Give students the time, date, and details for next week's "Take It to the Streets" group project. Be sure to instruct them in the proper attire and to provide permission slips as necessary. You may want to make up a flyer they can take home that will provide the necessary information for them and their parents. Also be sure students know to be working on the Week 15 memory verse, five days of study, and three individual "X-treme Challenges," and the Week 13 individual Bible study over the next two weeks.

SESSION 14

"Taking It to the Streets" Compassion Project

Do something together as a group to share with others the compassion of Christ. Here are some suggestions:

- ⊘ Go to a homeless shelter and show compassion by helping to feed the homeless or doing whatever the shelter requests. Be sure you ask your students to interact one-on-one with those using the shelter. Maybe set a goal of conversation and interaction with at least two people. You could perhaps take little gift packs—toothbrush, toothpaste, tissues, and so forth—and include with each a note about Jesus' love.
- ⊘ Go to a nursing home and show compassion to those who are elderly. You may want to ask the nurses to identify the persons who have few visitors and focus on those. Challenge your students to physically touch or hug those who live there. You could give each of those you visit a small gift with a note attached about Jesus and his love for them.
- ⊘ Hand out blankets to the homeless with a note about Jesus' love attached to them.
- ⊘ Go to a busy intersection and hand out free soft drinks or cold water on a hot day with a note about Jesus' love.

There are a lot of things you could to do to show Christ's compassion. Be creative!

After your project is done, take your students to a quiet place and debrief the experience with them. Do this immediately afterwards instead of waiting until your next group session. Here are some questions use can use (feel free to add your own):

- 🗨 What stood out to you as we worked together?
- 🗨 What was really meaningful about this experience?
- 🗨 How did you feel before we went?
- 🗨 How did you feel after we finished?

- Did you really feel you were making a difference? If not, what could have been done differently?
- How do you think Jesus felt about our mission?

Before your students take off, remind them that you will be checking their Week 15 journal assignments (including the memory verse, the five days of study, and the three individual "X-treme Challenges") and their notes from their individual Bible study at your next group session.

Understanding Your Life Mission: Leadership

OBJECTIVES

- To examine scriptural characteristics of a leader.
- To think about questions the group would ask a godly leader.
- To pray for each other to be the leaders God desires.

Resources Needed

Index cards, pens or pencils

Chalkboard or dry erase board

Poster board or butcher paper, markers

Bibles

Paper

Student journals

Session 15

Using My Gifts—Making a Difference

Warm Up

Give each student an index card with *one* characteristic of a leader written on it. Some of the characteristics you could write on the cards are *honest, wise, patient, loyal, humble, passionate, self disciplined, courageous,* and *generous.* Ask each person in the group to tell why his or her characteristic is most important to being a leader. If you have ten or more students, split into two groups and reuse some of the characteristics. If you have three or fewer students, give each person multiple cards.

After everyone has a chance to defend their characteristics, take a vote on which one is the least important. (You can name the characteristics one by one and ask persons to raise their hands to vote that characteristic off. The one with the most votes is out.) If there is a tie, flip a coin to break it. After the first round, repeat the process by having everyone vote again. Continue until there are only two characteristics left, then discuss the following:

- Was it tough to decide what the most important characteristics of a leader are?
- Why did you reject the characteristics you did?
- *Can a person just have a few of these qualities and still be a good leader?* Yes, but probably not the leader God wants him or her to be.

Say, *Today we will focus on important characteristics of a godly leader.*

Checking the Gear

Have students recite the Week 15 memory verse (1 Timothy 4:12) and make sure they completed the five days of study, the three individual "X-treme Challenges," and the individual Bible study. Spend some time eliciting specific feedback about the "X-treme Challenges." Were they difficult or uncomfortable to do? What feelings did they bring up? What was learned? Taking time to thoroughly process spiritual exercises and experiences will go a long way toward helping to bring about change and growth in the lives of your students.

Starting the Course

One of your students' "X-treme Challenges" was to have a "positive only" day, during which they were to speak only positive things to others. Ask, *How did that go? Was it hard to relate to some people? Did you have to change any of your regular communication patterns?* Students were also to evaluate the things they see, hear, say, and do for three days to see whether they are living a life of purity. Ask, *What did you discover? Were you surprised at what you found out about your "intake" and "output"?* Finally, students were challenged to make a prayer list and to record on that list the times and instances when God answered their prayers. Ask those who are willing to share about any answers they received.

Say, *Don't give up on speaking positively and living purely; God will continue to help you. And don't give up praying; God is faithful!*

Running the Course

Say, *Let's do some in-depth study of God's expectations of leaders.* Divide the class into twos or threes. (If your group is three or less, keep everyone together.) Give each group a poster board or a sheet of butcher paper and some markers. Groups should look up the following scriptures and write down all the qualifications of a leader that they find there. Write these scriptures on the board; the leadership qualifications students should find are given in parentheses:

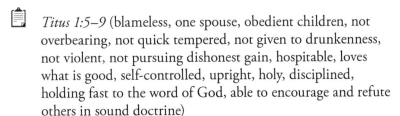 *Titus 1:5–9* (blameless, one spouse, obedient children, not overbearing, not quick tempered, not given to drunkenness, not violent, not pursuing dishonest gain, hospitable, loves what is good, self-controlled, upright, holy, disciplined, holding fast to the word of God, able to encourage and refute others in sound doctrine)

 *Acts 6:1–7* (full of the Holy Spirit, full of wisdom, full of faith)

 1 Timothy 3:1–10 (in addition to the Titus passage: above reproach, respectable, able to teach, gentle, not quarrelsome, not a lover of money, good repetition with outsiders, not a brand new Christian)

After the groups are finished, ask them to display their charts and to explain what they found. Ask, *Why do you think God is so concerned about leaders and the qualities they possess?* He knows that the leader is critical to the direction the people go. If the leader is not right with God, he or she will lead the people in a direction away from God and damage a lot of lives.

Say, *It is a great honor—and a great responsibility—to be called to Christian leadership.*

Finishing the Course

In their small groups, students should take paper and come up with some questions they would like to ask an experienced, godly leader about leadership. These could be questions dealing with how to lead others publicly or personal questions on how to live a godly life. Encourage students to be creative. Each group should come up with at least five and no more than ten.

After a few minutes, bring the groups back together and collect the lists; these will be useful for the Session 16 "Taking It to the Streets" Leadership Project. If you wish, make copies of all the questions and give each student a complete set; this resource could then be useful to them in the future in dialoging with leaders about the leadership they provide.

Cooling Down

Go around the group and ask each person to choose either what they *see, hear, say,* or *do* as the area they most need to work on to be the leaders God wants them to be. If you have a large group, ask each student to pair up and to pray for one another for this need. If your group is small, you may want to gather around and lay hands on each person, praying for the areas that are identified.

Give students the time, date, and details for next week's "Take It to the Streets" group project. Be sure to instruct them in the proper attire and to provide permission slips as necessary. You may want to make up a flyer they can take home that will provide the necessary information for them and their parents. Also be sure students know to be working on the Week 17 memory verse, five days of study, and three individual "X-treme Challenges," and the Week 15 individual Bible study over the next two weeks.

SESSION 16

"Taking It to the Streets" Leadership Project

Do something together as a group to help your students grow in their understanding of godly leadership and in their own leadership skills. Here are some suggestions:

- ⊘ Contact one or two respected spiritual leaders and arrange to go to their home or office for a question and answer time (maybe a pastor, church elder, and so forth). You can use some of the questions your group came up with during Session 15. (It may be nice to provide the questions beforehand so these leaders can prepare to answer in more depth.)
- ⊘ Have the group observe someone they consider a good leader during the week (pastor, teacher, parent, coach, and so forth). Have them write down some information about how these people act and behave. Have them talk to these leaders and ask some of the questions your group has come up with. Meet together in a week to discuss what students experienced and how it can apply to the group and their lives.
- ⊘ Make arrangements to spend time with someone in elected secular leadership (mayor, city council member, or even a state or national government representative, if possible; many people in these leadership positions will be glad to host your group and give you a tour of their offices. Ask students to take notes on what they learn and observe. Afterwards, discuss with your students any signs they see of godly leadership with these individuals, and how godly leadership could benefit someone in such a role.

After your project is done, take your students to a quiet place and debrief the experience with them. Do this immediately afterwards instead of waiting until your next group session. Here are some questions you can use (feel free to add your own):

- 🗨 What stood out to you as we worked together?
- 🗨 What was really meaningful about this experience?
- 🗨 How did you feel before we went?
- 🗨 How did you feel after we finished?
- 🗨 Did you really feel you were making a difference? If not, what could have been done differently?
- 🗨 How do you think Jesus felt about our mission?

Before your students take off, remind them that you will be checking their Week 17 journal assignments (including the memory verse, the five days of study, and the three individual "X-treme Challenges") and their notes from their individual Bible study at your next group session.

SESSION 17

Understanding Your Life Mission: Making a Difference

OBJECTIVES

- To examine characteristics in Jesus' life that made a difference in the lives of others.
- To examine what characteristics we need to impact others.
- To come up with practical ways to make a difference in others' lives.
- To pray that God will use your students to make a difference in other's lives.

Resources Needed

Chalkboard or dry erase board

Index cards, pens or pencils

Bibles

Paper

Student journals

Session 17

Understanding Your Life Mission: Making a Difference

Warm Up

Distribute index cards and ask each student to write the names of three people who have had a positive impact in his or her life and why these individuals made a difference. After a few minutes, invite students to share who they thought of and why. Try to find main themes that run through their answers, such as character, time invested with them, encouragement, and so forth.

Point out that the things Jesus did and the way he lived and how it has changed millions and millions of lives. As his followers, he equips *us* to make a difference in the lives of those we are around. Say, *Today we'll investigate what it really means to make a difference.*

Checking the Gear

Have students recite the Week 15 memory verse (Colossians 3:17) and make sure they completed the five days of study, the three individual "X-treme Challenges," and the individual Bible study. Spend some time eliciting specific feedback about the "X-treme Challenges." Were they difficult or uncomfortable to do? What feelings did they bring up? What was learned? Taking time to thoroughly process spiritual exercises and experiences will go a long way toward helping to bring about change and growth in the lives of your students.

Starting the Course

One of your students' "X-treme Challenges" was to fast from a meal and to pray during that time that God would use them to make a difference in the lives of others. Ask, *How did that go? Did you find it difficult to fast? Did God speak anything to your heart?* Review with your students Acts 4:32–37. Ask, Why do you think Barnabas was called "son of encouragement"? What did he do to make a difference in the lives of others? What do you think he did to prepare to make a difference in this way? Invite students to respond.

Say, *We don't know exactly what Barnabas did to prepare, but it's evident he had a heart that was open and sensitive to the things of God.*

Running the Course

Have a scripture hunt to see who can find instances in the Bible where Jesus made a difference in someone's life. Provide paper and give students ten or so minutes to look through the Gospels (Matthew, Mark, Luke, and John) to find these life-changing situations. If you have four or more students, divide them into groups of two. If you have three or less, let everyone stay together.

After time is up, bring the groups back together and ask them to report on what they found. (There is no shortage of instances where Jesus made a difference—that's what he spent his life doing!) Ask your students to identify some characteristics in Jesus' life that helped him make a difference; summarize these on the board. Some possible answers include *compassion, love, integrity, consistency,* and so forth. Challenge students to think of characteristics *we* need to have in order to make a positive difference in the lives of others. These should be the same as those shown by Jesus.

Say, *Jesus gave us a strong example of how to make a difference in the lives of others.*

Finishing the Course

Have your students form groups of three to five. (If you have less than five students, you may want to all stay together to work on this exercise.) From the list of characteristics you just made, ask your students to come up with some practical ways they could put them into practice. Provide paper for students to record their ideas. (You may wish to collect these to use with the Session 18 Group Project.)

Say, *Making a difference does not have to be complicated; it happens one day and one life at a time.*

Cooling Down

Pray with your students that God will use them to make a difference in someone's life. You may want to pray specifically by name for people your group has in mind. You may also want to pray that God will develop the characteristics of Christ in you as a part of this endeavor.

You should already have plans in place for doing a concluding activity during Session 20. Before you depart, discuss the details of this activity and make sure your students know that it's coming up in three weeks (next week there will be a "Taking It to the Streets" group project, then the following week will be the last classroom session). Make the class aware of the date, the starting time and the duration of the activity, the cost involved, appropriate dress for the occasion, any necessary equipment that will be needed, any parental permission slips that may be required, and so on.

Give students the time, date, and details for next week's "Take It to the Streets" group project. Be sure to instruct them in the proper attire and to provide permission slips as necessary. You may want to make up a flyer they can take home that will provide the necessary information for them and their parents. Also, be sure students know to be working on the Week 19 memory verse, five days of study, and three individual "X-treme Challenges," and the Week 17 individual Bible study over the next two weeks.

SESSION 18

"Taking It to the Streets" Making a Difference Project

Do something together as a group to make a difference in someone's life. You can probably use some of the ideas students generated in Session 17. Here are some possibilities:

- ✓ Ask those involved in your church's children's ministry if there are any children who need special attention. Have a party for them or take them to the park as a group.
- ✓ If your group consists entirely of high schoolers, do something with the middle school students in your church. Maybe ask them to go to the mall or somewhere else with your group.
- ✓ If you live in the city, contact an inner-city ministry; if you live in a rural area, contact someone who works with social services in your area. Ask if there are any opportunities for you to spend time with children who need some extra attention.

For any of the above suggestions, the best-lasting impact would come from an ongoing relationship with the children you spend time with. Think about a "big brother/big sister" type relationship, where students could have ongoing weekly or monthly contact.

After your project is done, take your students to a quiet place and debrief the experience with them. Do this immediately afterwards instead of waiting until your next group session. Here are some questions use can use (feel free to add your own):

- 💬 What stood out to you as we worked together?
- 💬 What was really meaningful about this experience?
- 💬 How did you feel before we went?
- 💬 How did you feel after we finished?
- 💬 Did you really feel you were making a difference? If not, what could have been done differently?
- 💬 How do you think Jesus felt about our mission?

Before your students take off, remind them that you will be checking their Week 19 journal assignments (including the memory verse, the five days of study, and the three individual "X-treme Challenges") and their notes from their individual Bible study at your next group session.

Understanding Your Life Mission: Growing

OBJECTIVES

- To understand the mission God has for us in regard to leadership (influence).
- To understand that growth is a natural and healthy part of maturing—including in our spiritual lives.
- To pray and commission each person in the group to become the leader God wants him or her to be.

Resources Needed

Old artifacts from your students' lives

Chalkboard or dry erase board

Paper, pens or pencils

Bibles

Student journals

Beginning the Climb Leader's Guides

Session 19

Understanding Your Life Mission: Growing

Warm Up

Before this session, collect from your students' parents some artifacts from the students' childhood—old photos, baby shoes, toys, and so forth. If you can't get something for every student, that's okay; just make sure you have a good representation. Be sure your students don't know that you're doing this. One at a time show the items you have brought. Ask, *Who do you think this is in this picture?* or, *Who did this belong to?* Point out to your students how much they have grown and matured over the years; they now look very little like their baby pictures, they can no longer fit in their baby clothes, and they no longer wish to play with their baby toys.

Say, *As children get older, they grow and mature; when that doesn't happen, something's wrong.*

Checking the Gear

Have students recite the Week 15 memory verse (Matthew 20:26–28) and make sure they completed the five days of study, the three individual "X-treme Challenges," and the individual Bible study. Spend some time eliciting specific feedback about the "X-treme Challenges." Were they difficult or uncomfortable to do? What feelings did they bring up? What was learned? Taking time to thoroughly process spiritual exercises and experiences will go a long way toward helping to bring about change and growth in the lives of your students.

Starting the Course

Review with your students the time logs they worked on from the first "X-treme Challenge" in Week 19 of their journals by discussing the following questions:

- Where did you end up spending most of your time?
- How did the time spent in your spiritual life compare to other areas of your life?
- Were you surprised at how much time you spent on some things?

Another "X-treme Challenge" was for students to plan out some goals and strategies in the *spiritual, family, ministry,* and *physical fitness* areas of their lives. Invite students to share some of the goals they came up with. Encourage them to share some from each of the four areas. This group is a good place for honest support and helpful suggestions with respect to these goals. (Are they challenging enough? Too challenging? How can the group members support one another in reaching these goals?)

Say, *Growth usually does not happen by accident; growth usually happens because it is intentional.*

Running the Course

In the completion of their five days of assignments for their journals, students studied five biblical leaders. Ask, *Can you remember the names of the Bible characters you studied and what you learned from each?* Day 1 looked at Joshua and getting our priorities right. Day 2 studied David and planning to succeed. Day 3 looked at Caleb and how to stay focused. Day 4 studied Josiah and what it means to grow as a leader. Day 5 studied Moses and how to deal with conflict. Discuss with your students which of these leaders stood out to them and why, and the things from these people's lives that we could apply today.

Say, *Each of these great leaders continued to grow in the pursuit of and in leadership skills.*

Finishing the Course

Read together Acts 6:6; 13:2–3. Ask, *How did the early church commission leaders?* In various places in the Bible, leaders were commissioned by the laying on of hands. Regardless of whether this class has been promoted and approached as being a "student leadership team" or not, point out to your students that they are, in fact, leaders; they have invested the time, the prayer, the Bible study, and the service to go above and beyond what many youth group members (and many adults in the church!) have done or would be willing to do. Say, *Today we will follow the biblical example in commissioning you to become the leaders God has prepared you to be.*

Create a "hot seat" by placing a chair in the middle of the room. Have one students sit here as the rest of the group gathers around and lays hands on this person. Ask someone to voice a prayer that this person will be the man or woman God has called him or her be and will develop into a strong spiritual leader. (It can add meaning to this ceremony of you invite your pastor, students' parents, or other significant adults to attend.) After praying for one individual, invite someone else to take the "hot seat" and pray for this person; continue until all students have been prayed for. Finish the time by having the students pray for you and your continued leadership.

Cooling Down

Give students the time, date, and details for next week's "Taking It to the Streets" concluding activity. Be sure to instruct them in the proper attire and to provide permission slips as necessary. You may want to make up a flyer they can take home that will provide the necessary information for them and their parents. Congratulate them on their pending completion of *Taking It to the Streets*; this is an accomplishment that is worth recognizing and celebrating with your whole church family. If your students have now completed all four levels of Ultimate Adventure Remix, they are worthy of a little extra congratulations and celebration.

Extra Challenge

You have been on an incredible journey with your students to help them grow spiritually. One of the best ways for them to continue that growth is for them to disciple others. You studied the fruit of the Spirit, but the fruit of a Christian is other Christians. If your students begin discipling others now, it can set a pattern that will last into adulthood.

Share with your students Matthew 28:19–20. Say, *Jesus instructed his disciples to go—and make disciples. What does this mean for us today?* These instructions are for us too as followers of Christ. Jesus wants us to help others grow spiritually. As your students continue the journey toward spiritual maturity and perfect Christlikeness, they should grab others and bring them along!

A great way for your students to begin discipling others would be to empower them to teach *Beginning the Climb* (Level 1 in the Ultimate Adventure Remix series) to other students. If this group is made up of all high school students, a great place to let them start would be with your middle school students. You might work with these new teachers the first time around so that they can learn from your model of teaching. Let them take some responsibility for experiential exercises in the first sessions and gradually hand off more of the responsibility, ending with their teaching most or all of the sessions at the end. These new teachers will also be the most effective recruiters for finding students who are eligible for *Beginning the Climb*.

If you are going to proceed with this plan, furnish each of your students a copy of the *Beginning the Climb: Leader's Guide* so they can begin familiarizing themselves with it. Pray that God will guide your teachers and send students to be discipled. Pray that those your teachers contact will be open to come to the group.

To order *Beginning the Climb*:   In USA, call toll-free: 800-741-7721.
Outside USA, call: 765-644-7721.
Order online: www.warnerpress.org.

SESSION 20

"Taking It to the Streets" Concluding Activity

Wrap up your time together in *Taking It to the Streets* by participating in a relevant interactive activity together. It would be ideal if you could take your students on a bike trip of significant length, but you can also take them to one of the following:

- ⊘ To an event that features biking or even motorcycle riding.
- ⊘ To a park, campground, or someplace where you can enjoy outdoor activities.
- ⊘ To help clean up or fix up the home of a disadvantaged family or a section of your city or community.
- ⊘ To do yard work for someone who is homebound.
- ⊘ To assist at a local shelter or food bank.
- ⊘ To paint the home of an elderly congregation member.

Whatever activity you choose, try to plan something that requires teamwork and cooperation. Even a pizza or pool party could suffice if you are intentional about celebrating your students' spiritual development and the ways in which their shared life in Christ has been deepened by this series.

ABOUT THE AUTHORS

Dr. Andy Stephenson has served as the leader of the youth and family ministries at Church of God Ministries (Anderson, IN) for the Church of God in North America since 2001. Andy is passionate about teenagers and seeing God use them to change their world. Andy speaks to youth and youth leaders in various settings across the globe and is focused on helping raise up a new generation of Christ-centered leaders.

He is an author and has taught at the university level since 2001. He married the love of his life, Candace, in 2005, and they have a little daughter named Mackenzie, born in 2007.

Andy holds a undergraduate degree from Mid-America Christian University in Bible and behavioral science, a master's degree from Oklahoma State University in marriage and family therapy, and a Ph.D. from the University of Texas at Arlington specializing in non-profit leadership.

Andy strongly believes in partnering with churches and youth workers to raise up a new generation of Christ-centered leaders. He has given his life and dedicated his gifts to that end.

Rick Winford has been teaching and ministering to young people since 1991. His great passion is to see teenagers develop their own relationship with God and not depend on their parents' religion. He holds a degree in religious studies from Anderson University and is currently employed in the high-tech industry, traveling all over the world in that role. His wife Peggy and son Andy continually make his life enjoyable.

CPSIA information can be obtained
at www.ICGtesting.com
Printed in the USA
LVHW050536210820
663773LV00022B/2789